Wallace "Famous" Amos

by Sarah L. Schuette

Consulting Editor: Gail Saunders-Smith, PhD

Consultant: Miles Smayling, PhD
Professor of Management
Minnesota State University, Mankato

CAPSTONE PRESS
a capstone imprint

Pebble Books are published by Capstone Press,
1710 Roe Crest Drive, North Mankato, Minnesota 56003
www.capstonepub.com

Library of Congress Cataloging-in-Publication Data
Schuette, Sarah L., 1976–
Wallace "Famous" Amos / by Sarah L. Schuette.
pages cm. — (Pebble books. Business leaders)
Includes bibliographical references and index.
Summary: "Simple text and photographs present the life of Wallace Amos, founder of Famous
Amos cookies"— Provided by publisher.
ISBN 978-1-4765-9639-6 (library binding)
ISBN 978-1-4765-9643-3 (paperback)
ISBN 978-1-4765-9647-1 (eBook PDF)
1. Amos, Wally—Juvenile literature. 2. Famous Amos Chocolate Chip Cookie Corporation—
Juvenile literature. 3. Businesspeople—United States—Biography—Juvenile literature. 4. Cookie
industry—United States—Juvenile literature. I. Title.
HD9058.C65A467 2014
338.7'6647525—dc23
[B]   2013035616

Note to Parents and Teachers

The Business Leaders set supports national social studies standards
related to people, places, and environments. This book describes
and illustrates Wallace "Famous" Amos. The images support
early readers in understanding the text. The repetition of words
and phrases helps early readers learn new words. This book also
introduces early readers to subject-specific vocabulary words,
which are defined in the Glossary section. Early readers may need
assistance to read some words and to use the Table of Contents,
Glossary, Read More, Internet Sites, and Index sections of the book.

Printed in the United States of America in North Mankato, Minnesota.
092013   007764CGS14

Table of Contents

Tallahassee, Florida in 1937

1936

born

Early Years

Chocolate-chip cookie maker Wallace "Wally" Amos was born July 1, 1936, in Tallahassee, Florida. His family did not have much money.

New York City in 1941

1936
born

1948
moves to New York

At age 12, Wally went to live with his Aunt Della in New York. She baked chocolate-chip cookies. Wally learned to love baking from his aunt.

Wally went to the Food Trades Vocational High School in the 1950s

1936
8   born

1948
moves to New York

1953
joins U.S. Air Force

Working Hard

Wally went to a high school that taught cooking skills. Then in 1953, Wally joined the U.S. Air Force. Wally moved back to New York in 1957. He was a hard worker.

Wally worked with The Supremes in the 1960s.

1936 born

1948 moves to New York

1953 joins U.S. Air Force

1962 becomes talent agent

In 1962 Wally became
a talent agent for musicians.
He worked with many singers.
Wally helped make them
famous. He started to bake
cookies for the many friends
he made.

Wally in 2000

1936
12 born

1948
moves to New York

1953
joins U.S.
Air Force

1962
becomes
talent agent

Businesses

Wally moved to Los Angeles in 1967. He opened a store there to sell his bite-size chocolate-chip cookies in 1975. The cookies were called "Famous Amos." People liked Wally's cookies.

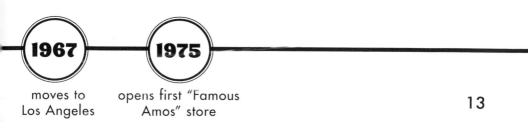

1967 moves to Los Angeles

1975 opens first "Famous Amos" store

13

1936
born

1948
moves to New York

1953
joins U.S.
Air Force

1962
becomes
talent agent

Wally sold his cookie company in 1985. In 1992 Wally started a new company to sell muffins and cakes. It is called Uncle Wally's Muffin Company.

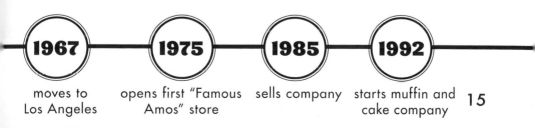

1967	1975	1985	1992
moves to Los Angeles	opens first "Famous Amos" store	sells company	starts muffin and cake company

1936

16 born

1948

moves to New York

1953

joins U.S.
Air Force

1962

becomes
talent agent

Encouraging Others

Wally believes reading is important. He encourages kids to stay in school. He gives money to reading programs. Wally believes in reading to kids every day.

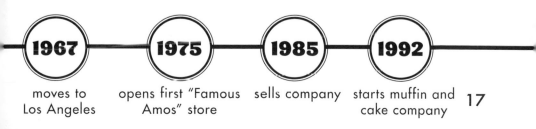

1967	1975	1985	1992
moves to Los Angeles	opens first "Famous Amos" store	sells company	starts muffin and cake company

1936 born

1948 moves to New York

1953 joins U.S. Air Force

1962 becomes talent agent

Wally is a good salesman and speaker. He has written many books. He speaks to businesses to help them work better. In his speeches Wally encourages others to keep a positive attitude.

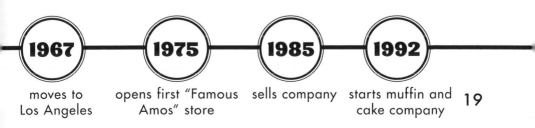

1967	1975	1985	1992
moves to Los Angeles	opens first "Famous Amos" store	sells company	starts muffin and cake company

1936
born

1948
moves to New York

1953
joins U.S.
Air Force

1962
becomes
talent agent

In 1980 one of Wally's Hawaiian shirts was given to the Smithsonian Museum in Washington, D.C. Today Wally's face and name still help sell millions of cookies. He still likes baking them too.

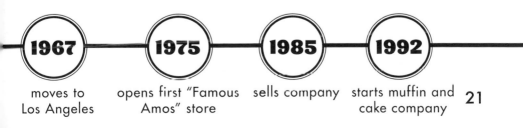

1967	1975	1985	1992
moves to Los Angeles	opens first "Famous Amos" store	sells company	starts muffin and cake company

Glossary

attitude—the way a person feels about something

encourage—to give praise and support

musician—a person who plays, sings, or writes music

program—an effort to help other people improve their lives

talent agent—a person who helps actors, singers, and other entertainers get work

Critical Thinking Using the Common Core

1. In his speeches Wally encourages others to have a positive attitude. What does it mean to have a positive attitude? Why do you think having a positive attitude is important? (Integration of Knowledge and Ideas)

2. Look at the photo on page 16. What is happening in this picture? What are some of the clues you used in the photo and the text to find your answer? (Craft and Structure)

3. Look at the timeline and the text. What are two jobs Wally had before he started selling his chocolate-chip cookies? (Key Ideas and Details)

Read More

Bredeson, Carmen. *The Chocolate Chip Cookie Queen: Ruth Wakefield and Her Yummy Invention.* Inventors at Work! Berkeley Heights, N.J.: Enslow Elementary, 2014.

Nelson, Robin. *From Cocoa Bean to Chocolate.* Food. Minneapolis: Lerner Publications Company, 2013.

Price, Pam. *Cool Cookies and Bars: Easy Recipes for Kids to Bake.* Cool Baking. Edina, Minn.: ABDO Pub. Co., 2010.

Internet Sites

FactHound offers a safe, fun way to find Internet sites related to this book. All of the sites on FactHound have been researched by our staff.

Here's all you do:

Visit *www.facthound.com*

Type in this code: 9781476596396

Check out projects, games and lots more at
www.capstonekids.com

23

Index

Word Count: 258
Grade: 1
Early-Intervention Level: 20

Editorial Credits
Michelle Hasselius, editor; Lori Bye, designer; Tracy Cummins, media researcher;
Jennifer Walker, production specialist

Photo Credits
Capstone Press: Karon Dubuke, 1, 14; Florida State Archives: Florida Memory, 4; Getty
Images: Apic, 6, Redferns, 10, Tom Williams/Roll Call, 18; Globe Photo, cover; LGBT
Community Center National History Archive, 8; Newscom: EMILIO FLOREZ, 12; Rex
USA: LINDA MATLOW, 20; Shutterstock: Apostrophe, cover background, Fomichova Olena,
cover background; U.S. Navy photo by Mass Communication Specialist 2nd Class Lindsay
Switzer, 16